"He's Sweet I Know"

The Life, Love and Legacy of
Apostle Christine Morris

Bloomingdale, IL

"Fight the good fight of faith, lay hold on eternal life, whereunto thou art also called, and has professed a good profession before many witnesses."

(I Timothy 6:12)

Apostle Christine Morris

"He's Sweet I Know"

The Life, Love & Legacy of
Apostle Christine Morris

King James Version: Scripture quotations marked "KJV" are taken from the Holy Bible, King James Version, Cambridge, 1769.

"Scripture quotations taken from the Amplified® Bible, Copyright © 1954, 1958, 1962, 1964, 1965, 1987 by The Lockman Foundation Used by permission." (www.Lockman.org)

Scripture taken from the Holy Bible, New International Version®, NIV® Copyright © 1973, 1978, 1984, 2011 by Biblica, Inc.™ Used by permission. All rights reserved worldwide.

All rights reserved.

No portion of this book may be reproduced or transmitted in any form or by any means, electronic or mechanical, including photocopying, recording, or by any information storage, without permission in writing from the author.

Printed in the Unites States of America.

ISBN Number: 978-0-9833697-4-5

LCCN: 2012945576

Copyright © 2012

McClure Publishing, Inc.
Bloomingdale, IL 60108
800-659-4908

"Exalt her, and she shall promote thee: she shall bring thee to honour, when thou dost embrace her."
                                                     (Proverbs 4:8)

To God, the Father, the Son and the Holy Ghost;

for saving my life a long time ago. I could never thank You enough for all that You have done for me, and how You have brought me through all that I have been through. Because of Your Grace and Your Mercy, I can forever give You the honor and the glory, and I will forever be grateful for my life. Thank You Jesus!

To my late husband, Bishop James Morris;

I thank God for you listening to the voice of God. Because you listened to God, I became your loving and faithful wife, and I am so glad that you did. THANK GOD! You taught me so much through your life, and now, the vision and ministry God gave you has continued to live on because of your obedience.

To my beloved mother, the late Mother Henrietta Williams;

I truly thank God for my mother. She taught me SO much, and she loved me SO much. I thank God for your life because you taught me from a little girl how to be a woman. I thank God for your life everyday.

To my beautiful daughter, Bernice;

You are truly a blessing to me. You have been SO good to me, and I thank God for you. I knew God had a special calling on your life even when you were a little girl. Words STILL cannot express how much I love you and thank God for you everyday of my life. Because of you, God has blessed my life in so many ways that I cannot count them all. Through your life, you gave me such a beautiful family: Reggie (deceased), Karen, Chris and Marcie; then you gave me Christina, Jasmine, Steve, Evan, Lil' Chris, Corey and all my other great-great grandchildren. Through your life, you gave me my family. I thank God for you.

Special Thanks to Minister Cortez
and Missionary Jeri Mack;

It gives me great pleasure to speak a word of thanks to them. God put it upon their hearts to support me in my vision to write my first book that God gave me many years ago. Minister Cortez said, *"Apostle, it is time for you to publish your first book"*. PRAISE THE LORD! So, I knew it was time to fulfill my dream. The Lord not only inspired me and motivated me, but He also encouraged me. Now, I pronounce blessings upon this family. I can hear the sound of the abundance of rain. God is sending an overflow upon these two people. I cannot reward you for your good works, but the Lord is going to do it. *"He that receiveth a prophet in the name of a prophet shall receive a prophet's reward;..."* (Matthew 10:41a)

Love, Apostle Dr. Christine Morris

- Table of Contents -

Chapter I: Her Life
"I Don't Know What I Would Do Without The Lord"

Born In Sin, But Shapen in Iniquity 19
Moving to Chicago 25
Why Should I Marry Him.. 35

Chapter II: Her Love
"Down Through The Years"

The Church and Its Purpose 47
Prayer and Fasting 51
The Truth About the Prophet
  and the Prophetess..59
The Apostle and the Apostleship............................ 63
The Beast and His Bride 65
Practical Nuggets of Wisdom 69
  - Our Christian Relationship
  - Addiction

Chapter III: Her Legacy
"He's Sweet I Know"

The Church History: First Pentecostal................... 79
My Family.. 83
Speak the Truth Fellowship..................................... 87
The Passing of the Torch... 89
Reflections of My Life.. 93

PREFACE

January 16, 2007

I am praising the Lord for blessing me to begin to put together the content of my first book which has been in my heart since September 15, 1960.

I went to bed that night and while I was asleep, God gave me a vision of the church world, and God said that the church world must wake up. In that vision of the church world, I saw two chairs. I was on the Adult Choir on the same level of the pulpit, and there were three large choirs, and three leaders sitting in those three chairs. It was our beloved bishop, the late Bishop James Morris, and his two assistant pastors. Down the steps right in front of the pulpit was the Offering Table. There stood a real tall man a microphone in his hands, and he looked at the pulpit, and said, "*Shoot!*" So, when he said, "*Shoot!*", someone rolled a pair of small black and white dice.

By me sitting in the choir, I could see the dice real good. I asked a lady sitting next to me, "*Were those dice?*", and she said, "*No!*". So, after that, the man with the microphone said, "*Shoot!*", and someone rolled a pair of dice again. They were a large pair of red and white dice. By us sitting in the choir stand, we were able to see the dice real plain. After this happen, I said to the person that was sitting next to me, "*I told you those were dice!*". I heard one of the sisters say to her husband, "*I was wondering what you were waiting on?*"

We began to leave the choir stand. We came down the steps next to the offering table because after the rolling of those dice, a curtain fell on the altar. It was a veil curtain. I could see the faces of the saints, Missionary L. Jones and Sister Georgia Mae Thomas. There were many of them struggling under the veil and at the same time, this big dark man with the microphone grabbed my arm and said, "*Let's get married?*", and I replied, "*No way!*" Then, he began to twist my arm so hard that he hurt me so bad. So, I said, "*Go and get my purse out of the choir stand*". As he started up the steps to get my purse, we began to run down the side of the aisle toward the front door. But when we made it out of the doors to the street, there were well dressed men coming towards us. They were dressed in black and white suits. They had gotten out of those big black cars. They too were our enemies. As they were coming towards us, I turned in the alley and ran out of the alley at 14th Street and Ashland Avenue. I ran so fast down Ashland Avenue in high heels that I did not stumble, and my hair was bound back. Where I was running, it was dark, I mean it was really dark, but Jesus was right at the break of day!

As I was running, I woke up or came out of the vision. I was in my twin bed, and I rolled out of the bed to the floor with my face down, and I could not speak. Tears began to fall from my eyes, my strength was limp. Somehow, I made it to the bathroom and I laid my head next to the bathtub. The tears continue to run down my face, and I began to pray, "*Oh God save me and save your people!*", . . . "*Oh, Lord God, save me and save your people!*" And the Lord said, "*I did! I woke you up, now the church world must wake up!*"

Praise the Lord!

The next morning when my daughter Bernice got up, and she was getting ready for school, she said, "*Mother, what happened last night? This house is weird.*" Then, I said to Bernice, "*I had a very bad dream last night.*" After I finished telling her about the dream, she left for school and I got ready for Bible Class. In those days, the church had Bible Class and Prayer everyday of the week, Monday through Friday services for three years. I had gotten to Bible Class. So, that morning as I made my way to church, I was weak in my body. So, after we were sitting around the table with the saints, our Bishop's wife asked me, "*Sister Fields, how do you feel?*" I said, "*Alright*", but I wanted to say that I had a dream, but she put her finger over my mouth and shook her head. So, I didn't say anything else about what I had dreamt. But after the Morning Class was over, Bishop's wife said to me, "*Sister Fields, would you carry my books upstairs?*", and I said, "*Yes Ma'am!*" When we made it upstairs, she told me to have a seat at the dining room table. So, when I sat down at the dining room table, she went into the bathroom. And she came out, she said, "*Now tell me about your dream*", and I began telling her about the dream. She began to cry when I finished telling her. She said to me, "*Sister Fields, that was not a dream, but a vision and it was going to come to pass"*. And I said to her, "*I don't want it to come to pass.*" Then she talked about the scripture in Habakkuk 2:2, where God said to the prophet Habakkuk, "*Write the vision, and make it plain*".

Mother, our Bishop's wife, said to me, "*Sister Fields, the saints have prayed for your strength. I want you to go home and lie down, and rest. And when your daughter comes home from school, have her write the vision and then you come over here and read it to your Bishop, the Pastor*". She said to come over here around five o'clock. So, after school, Bernice came home and I told her what Mother told me to do, and asked her would she help me, and would she do the writing and she said, "*Yes Mom*". So, we went to the kitchen table and began writing. As we started, all of a sudden, something began happening to us. We both became confused in our words. It was a spirit of Satan and it looked as though a real shadow was in the north corner of our living room. We began praying in the Spirit of the Lord, and pleading the Blood of Jesus Christ. The shadows left the rooms of our house, "*Praise the Lord for the victory through the Blood.*" Then, we were able to finish writing the vision.

Then, both of us made our way to see our Bishop just as his wife instructed me earlier that day. So, when we got there, our Bishop was resting in his chair over by the window. Mother said, "*Elder Morris, . . . Sister Fields and her daughter Bernice is here to see you. She came over to read something to you*". He spoke to us and said, "*Alright, you all read it*". He also said, "*Give it to Sister Sullivan, and let her read it*". So one of us gave her the vision that was written on paper and she began to read . . .

. . . . . the vision!

Chapter I: Her Life
"*I Don't Know What I Would Do Without the Lord*"

Born In Sin, But Shapen In Iniquity

My beloved Mother, begotten me by my father, Mr. Joe Lark on May 9, 1927. My Mother was married at the time to Mr. Turner Johnson. So, after I was born, Mr. Turner said to my Mother, "*That baby is not my baby. That's Joe's baby, so give her to him*". Of course Papa was married, too, but he agreed to take me home to his wife. She had four other children, but she took care of me. I did not know my real Mother until I was around six years old. At Christmas time, this little lady would come to visit us. But I did not think or know that she was my Mother.

So, at the age of six years old, this beautiful young lady came at Christmas time. But this time, right after dinner, I heard her ask my father could she take me home with her. In turn, my father said to me, "*Do you want to go home with Henrietta? No Papa*", I said. Then he said, "*This is your Mother*". I said, "*Papa, I don't want her to be my Mother. Mama Mae Jane is my Mother.*" But he said, "*No, I want you to go home with her because you have other sisters at her house*". So, when he made that statement, I willingly agreed to go home with her. And at sunset, we said goodbye to Papa and Mama Mae Jane. Papa put me on the back of a horse with my real Mother, Henrietta, and away we went. It was not long before I went to sleep, and that's all I remember until the next morning.

When I woke up, I could hear two girls talking. They were saying this is our little sister. One of them said, "*Look at her hair*", because I had such a beautiful head of hair. Then, one of them said, "*Look at her nose*". I came out from under the sheet and they said, "*Hey, what's your name?*" I said, "*My name is Christine*". I jumped out of bed and that was it. Not long after that, my Mother broke up with this man, Mr. Gene Bradford, the housekeeper. Unfortunately, I did not know her husband, Mr. Turner Johnson. Mother had three girls by him. But after Mother broke up housekeeping with her friend, Mr. Gene, she took us to live with her Mother's sister and our great grandmother.

Our Mother went on the road because she was a good cook. One day, her boss lady and her were traveling on the road and had a car accident. My Mother's arm was broken and her teeth were knocked out. So around six months later, they brought my Mother back home. We were glad to see Mother at home again. Not long after she came home, she got married to another man, and she moved us out of her Aunt's home in order to have a place for her children.

On Saturday night, my Mother got married to Mr. Bud Button. What a sacrifice for Mother to make so she could keep her girls together, that marriage did not last very long because that man was so jealous. One time, my sister Louise and I were playing up in the attic of the house where that man hid his shotgun. We were so afraid, and told Mother about what we had found, and she said, "*Go bring it to me*". She took the gun apart, piece by piece, . . . Thank God! So, a few days later, one night we heard noise coming from Mother's bedroom. Her husband ran to get that gun, but Mother had already taken it apart—broken it up.

Then Mother's husband ran outside and found a real large pole. When my Mother saw him coming back in the front door, she ran to close the door. But the man brought in that pole just before Mother could close the door and broke her arm. We were crying because we looked at Mother's arm, and it was hanging.

Mother ran to her boss because she was their housekeeper. They carried Mother to the hospital. We did not see our Mother for a while. But my father came and took us from that place. His boss brought him up there because her husband's boss did not want to let us move. He said that no one was coming to that place. But my father's boss, not only came to his place, but he moved everything that my Mother had. My father, Mr. Joe Lark, took me with him again. But he put my Mother and the others in a cookhouse so she could work for his boss. Where he took them was not far from where he lived. We could see each other everyday.

One evening Mama Mae Jane told me to go and take Papa some water. He was in the field working on a Friday afternoon. I carried the water to Papa, but he looked at me and said, "*What's wrong with you?*" I said, "*My head is hurting*". He said to me, "*Go and tell your Mother to give you something to take*". I did so, and she gave me some Castor Oil.

My father came to the house after he stopped working, and he took a bath and left the house. We did not see him again until Sunday evening. He would always come home on Sunday night in order to be ready for work on Monday morning. But whenever he would come home, he wanted to see all of his children.

As for me, I was still sick. He asked his wife, "*Where is that little nigger?*" That is what he called me, and she replied, "*She is around here somewhere*". I was under the table or under the bed trying to keep cool. I was so sick with a high fever.

Papa brought me out from under the "whatever" I was under, and he said, "*This child is burning up with a high fever*". I can see the hand of God in all this because He sent my father home. Papa ran to his boss' house for him to take us to the doctor and he did.

The doctor came and looked at me. Then he put his hand over my stomach and said, "*I think you better get her to the hospital as soon as you can because she has appendicitis*". Papa's boss put a mat on his pickup truck and started to drive as fast as he could taking me to the hospital that was in Grenada, Mississippi.

When we arrived at the hospital, they carried me in, and began to see what was wrong with me. After a while, they came and told my father what they found, but they could not take my appendix until the next day. They did not know if I would be alright or not. So, my father began to cry, and said to the hospital doctor, "*Don't let my nigger child die*".

They did surgery that night. I was eight years old at the time. My Mother was already sick with pneumonia when they told her what had happened to me. She cried so hard until Papa brought her to the hospital to see me, her baby.

After she got there to see me, they put my Mother in the same room with me, and she stayed right there in the hospital until they discharged me. Papa came to take care of us. Papa was a good man to his family.

After Mother and I recovered from our sicknesses, Mother began to keep company with a man by the name of Mr. Seth Williams. When they got married, I was nine years old. Mother moved in to the city. Before they were married, Mr. Seth was a hard working man. After he married Mother, he quit working at the Saw Mill, and the next thing I knew, we moved to Memphis, Tennessee because Mr. Seth got a job working on the road laying pipes. While still in Memphis, Mother worked as a beauty technician. Papa Seth sent for Mother to come where he was in Texas. At that time, I was living in Memphis, grown, married and had a beautiful little girl. Later in 1947, Papa Seth and Mother moved from Texas to Chicago, Illinois.

Moving to Chicago

My Mother brought me to Chicago to live because I was sick again. I was living in Indianapolis, Indiana in 1950, and had an operation. My Mother came to my house, packed my things and took me home with her. The doctor told my Mother that I wouldn't live and I was going to die. When the doctor told my Mother this, I was still in the hospital. She asked the doctor if she could take me out of the hospital, and the doctor's response was, *"What are you going to do with a dead woman?"* My Mother told the doctor that, *"the God she served said my child wouldn't die!"*. Oh, praise God, my mother was right. I didn't die. So, it was on that day my Mother took me out of the hospital.

Around 5:00 a.m. the next morning, my Poppa and Mama hit the highway coming to Chicago, Illinois. We arrived at 626 East 46th Street. When we got to the front building, my Mother yelled towards the window to get my Aunt Rose's attention. She told Aunt Rose to have someone to bring a chair downstairs for me. I was so weak in my body, I couldn't walk.

My Mother tended and cared for me for about three weeks. I slowly began to recover. She then took me to a doctor who said the only thing wrong with me was that my blood was low. My Mother then gave him the letter, which the doctor in Indianapolis, Indiana had given to her. After the Chicago doctor read the letter, he looked at my Mother and told her that is what he diagnosed. My Mother then told the doctor that she prayed. When she said, "*I prayed*", the doctor said to her, "*You did more than prayed. You need to be my nurse*".

After a while, I went back to Indianapolis, Indiana to live. I was doing well. In 1951, I gave myself a birthday party. My family came from Chicago. Believe me, I was up again, and this was my twenty-fifth birthday. However, I did not give God the praise for sparing my life, because I didn't know how. Even in all my ignorance, I was very prosperous. Within three years, I accomplished a lot of things and lived pretty well. So, I thought. I didn't know that sin was being added to sin.

I became sick again. This time I had to sell all my household goods and clothes just to be able to pay my doctor bill. Around the Fall of 1953, I ended up back in Chicago with my Mother. She and God got me back on my feet again. I still thought nothing of this. I got a job and moved out of my Mother's house again. I hired someone to keep my house while I worked.

The holidays were coming, so I contacted an old male from Indianapolis to come over for dinner. He came and did the cooking, spent the day with us, and left for home. But around midnight, I took sick again. This time, it was much worse than ever before. My Mother sat up at night with me because I couldn't sleep. She walked the floor with me, praying and crying out to God. Sometimes, it seemed like it was all night long. This went on for months and weeks.

I noticed that my Mother didn't look so good. We lived in a big house, and sometimes it was 21 people in that house. But only my Mother stayed up at night with me. She was beginning to get tired, but not enough to complain. I told my Mother to let me go down south so I could die in peace. There was no one to help my Mother. I felt like Job. The only thing different was, Job was not guilty of anything, but I was. I had unconfessed sin in my life.

After a while, my Mother asked me whom I would live with if I went down south. All of Momma's people had left the south. I don't know why I said this, but I told her I would live with Mother Alice. She was a Christian woman. In fact, she was the Aunt to Uncle Charlie who was married to my Mother's sister, A.P. My Momma agreed, and she contacted Mother Alice.

The next question was who was going to take me down to Mississippi. My cousin Annie Mae Suggs volunteered. Momma purchased two train tickets, and we boarded the train. Around midnight, I had a sick spell. I told Ann I had to go to the washroom. She asked me if I wanted her to go with me. I replied, "*No*", and I made it to the washroom. While I was sitting there, I looked out of the window with tears in my eyes. I saw a cross. At first, it was a moon, and then all at once, it changed into a cross. I came out of the washroom as fast as I could and went back to my seat. My cousin Ann put my head in her lap and I slept all the way to Mississippi.

We arrived in Mississippi around two in the morning. We stayed with an old couple who was my Mother's aunt and uncle. My uncle was blind, but they were both fine Christians. The next morning, Ann got us a ride out to the country where Mother Alice lived. She gladly received us into her home.

Of course, my Mother had agreed to pay her $12 a week to take care of me. For many a night and day, Mother Alice had her hands full. She was a praying woman, but without power. She was no match for those demonic powers that had a grip on me. As the Bible says, "*This kind comes out only by prayer and fasting.*" (Matthew 17:21) (Emphasis added)

I cannot recall the month or day that a lady and two children were on the pond fishing, not far from Mother Alice's house. It began to rain real hard, so they came to the house where I was staying. I don't remember when they came in because I was asleep. Whenever I had a sick spell, I would pass out. They would come on at 6:00a.m., . . . 9:00a.m., . . . 12:00p.m., . . . 3:00p.m., . . . 6:00p.m., . . . 9:00p.m. and midnight. When I woke up, I heard voices. I pulled the sheet from over my head. I saw a lady and two children. I didn't know them, but her name was Sister Pattie Lou Johnson. Sister Johnson spoke to me and asked me how long I had been sick. I told her a long time. Then, she asked me if I believed if they prayed for me that the Lord would heal me. I was very angry, so I said that God was able. Then she said she was not going to ask me, but was going to believe God for my healing.

The sun had come back out and she and her children left the house. But, each and every day she came by the house and read the Bible to me. She read Psalm 107:20, which said, *"He sent His Word and healed them, and delivered [them] from their destructions"*. After they prayed, I thanked Jesus that I never had another seizure from that day forth.

I began to get my strength back, and I started going in and out of doors. One day, I heard Ms. Esther tell Mother Alice that she didn't want that sanctified woman in her yard. Mother Alice told Ms. Esther that Sister Pattie Johnson had done me so much good. Ms. Esther repeated herself. She didn't want that sanctified woman in her house or around her yard. These words made Mother Alice feel very sad. Mother Alice told me I had to tell Sister Pattie Johnson what Ms. Esther had said. When Sister Johnson came to read the scriptures and pray, I told her what Ms. Esther said. Sister Johnson wasn't even upset. She just said it was all right, because I had enough strength to walk to the mailbox. Thank God because I hadn't realized that I built up enough strength to go as far as the mailbox.

One day, Sister Pattie Johnson asked me if I would like to go home with her. I told her I had to ask Mother

Alice first. Mother Alice agreed right away. This time, Sister Johnson and her family came in a wagon. She put me upon it and we rode for a very long time.

In the meantime, before we arrived, Satan was setting up my mind. He was telling me I was a fool because they were going to *"fix"* me. These same people prayed me through to a healing. I told the devil that it was alright anyhow, because I was trying to get to God.

After the long ride, we arrived at a tent meeting. We got out and went in the meeting. No one said anything to me. They just set me on a bench. I had never been in a meeting like that before. They were singing songs I'd never heard before. When I came to myself, I was laying on the ground in sawdust. Not long afterwards, Sister Johnson told me we were going next door. We went into the house and they were serving ice cream and cooking. I was offered some, but refused to take it because I could never eat late at night before. The hostess told me it wouldn't hurt me. Thank You Jesus! I ate it and it was good.

After we finished eating, we got back on the wagon and went to Sister Pattie Johnson's house. It was very late when we got there, and her husband was asleep. She woke him up and introduced me as Henrietta's daughter. Lo, and behold, he was my mother's brother-in-law. This was my Sister Louise's uncle. Her father's brother was my mother's first husband's brother. *"Oh God, I truly thank you for how you brought me through"*. Uncle said he had heard I'd been sick. He told me he would see me in the morning.

They put me to bed, and thank God I slept all through the night. When I woke up the next morning, Sister Johnson came in my room and asked me what I wanted to eat for breakfast. I told her whatever they ate. She said they weren't going to eat until 4:00 p.m. because they were fasting for me. Believe me, I had never heard of fasting before then. I told Sister Johnson I wouldn't eat either.

They all left me alone in the house, and I began to wander around outside. When I came to myself, I was in the woods. That evil spirit began talking to me again. It said that snakes were going to bite me. I told that evil spirit I didn't care because God was going to help me. Listen, I didn't know God or Jesus because of the unconfessed sin in my life. But thanks be unto God for I know Him now because I repented of all my sins.

At that time, I wasn't afraid of a snake in the woods, but you can believe me when I say I was afraid of God. God was dealing with me in His mercy all the time, and I didn't know it. After the prayer that was prayed for me, it wasn't long before I started attending Sunday School with Mother Alice. We went to the Baptist Church, and I had strength enough now to stay all day. I must confess, I didn't understand, but I can tell anyone now that they must be born again.

In a little while, I was able to come back to Chicago with my family and my little girl. Thank You Jesus! My Mother was so glad I made it home again.

Before I left Mississippi, Sister Johnson gave me a sheet of paper with a lot of names on it. They were addresses of churches in Chicago. She wanted me to contact some of them so they could come and pick me up for church services. It was a while before I decided to call one of them.

I was taking a bath when it crossed my mind that my color was back and I was gaining weight. I came out of the bathroom, and said to my cousin, Rose Suggs that I hadn't shared what happened while I was down South. Then, I begin to tell her how Sister Pattie had prayed for me and I got well. Then I showed her the paper with all the church addresses on it. Sister Suggs told me to contact one and I did. Sure enough, the lady on the phone said that she would pick me up for church and she did – Thank God! She made herself known to me. Before the lady arrived, I told Rose not to tell my Mother where I was going. I gave Rose my jewelry box and chest and made her promise not to tell my Mother.

The lady arrived and we drove to a church on Bowen Street. The service was already in progress when we arrived. No one said anything to me. They didn't ask my name, or where I came from.

After the service, the Pastor asked if I wanted to be healed, and I responded, *"Yes Sir!"*. Some Church Mothers took me in the back. They opened a door to a room with a lot of white gowns. They put a gown on me and baptized me that night. The lady took me back home. I did not join the church that night.

When I got home, my Mother was waiting for me. She took me aside and told me that I couldn't live that (sanctified) kind of life. I must say that my Mother was born again and seemed to have religion. But did she have sanctification and holiness? Most of the leaders in her church were not teaching the members about sanctification or salvation. But later in life, my Mother did receive the fullness of God and the Holy Ghost. Thank You Jesus!

My Mother told me to put my jewelry on and fix myself up. I was obedient to what my Mother told me, but I moved out of her house eventually. This time, in 1953, I moved on Walnut Street on the West Side.

While I was on the West Side, I applied for low-income housing. When things got better, I moved back to the South Side on 41st and Drexel. However, in 1957, I received a letter to come to the housing projects at 1440 West 14th Street, Apt. 906. When I went to inspect the place, I fell in love with it. So did my Mother. I paid my rent that day and they gave me the keys to the apartment right then and there. Listen, God was in the plans.

After I moved in the apartment, it looked like I was becoming more settled in my mind, thank God! But one night, Satan upset me. He was trying to get me back on the south side with my old gang. Oh, God, I thank You! My Mother and Poppa had come over because I was so upset. But I didn't move. After that night, things got a little better because my Momma would always pray.

My daughter, Bernice was over to her grandmother's house, and I was home alone. But before that time, Bernice came in from the store and told me that we didn't have to go on the south side to church because there were quite a few churches in the back of our house.

She was right. There was Shiloh Baptist Church, Zion Hill Church and others, but God led us to the First Pentecostal Church of God. Thanks be unto God!

Why Should I Marry Him?

I am so blessed by the Lord and Saviour Jesus Christ. The Lord saved my soul in 1957, and He blessed me to leave all and live for Him.

After the Lord saved me things began to get very hard on this side of life. But God helped me with my thirteen-year-old daughter, Bernice, to finish school. Then the Lord blessed her to get a job at Spiegel's. Not long after that, she got married and moved out in her own house. Then the authority sent for me and said, *"Christine, you have to move out of your apartment because you do not have any small children in your home"*. At the same time, the Lord was working on my behalf.

When my Mother told my Poppa what happen, my Dad said, "*She can't come back here to stay with us at this time.*" I had no income at all. Marie, my older sister, said I could stay with her and her common law husband, Richard. They both made me feel very welcomed. So I moved in the back room. I spent most of my time on my knees crying out to God for help (Psalm 121:1-2).

I thank the Lord because He heard my cry

I did not believe in the way they lived, because they lived as husband and wife for many years and they were not legally married. I was not there very long, because in 1963, my life was going to change. It would change because of our Bishop James Morris of the First Pentecostal Church of God, Inc.

I went to church one morning and I was praying. Someone touched me on the shoulder and said, "*Sister Fields, the Pastor wants to see you*". I said to her, "*I wonder what he wants?*", and she replied to me, "*I guess he is going to move you from being the President of the Morning Bible Class*". After she walked away, I continued to pray on my knees. Then another lady touched my shoulder and said, "*Sister Fields, Bishop told me to tell you that he wants to see you*". Then I said to myself, "*I don't care what they say because I am leaving anyway because I'm a great evangelist!*" I had in my mind to go to another city to live.

Finally, I finished praying and went over to our Bishop Morris home. As I arrived at the door, I met two Evangelists coming out and they said, "*Come on in Sister Fields, Pastor is waiting for you.*" As I entered, he said, "*Come on in and have a seat.*"

In 1963, the Man of God said to me, "*Sister Fields, how do you feel about marriage?*" I said, "*Bishop, I think it's wonderful for these young people to get married.*" He replied, "*I'm not talking about the young people, but I'm talking about you. How do you feel about marriage?*" I said, "*I have been married before so, I don't think about it anymore.*" Our Bishop, Pastor James Morris said to me, "*Sister Fields, the reason I asked you about marriage is because the Lord said to me that you would be my next wife.*" I said to Bishop, "*The Lord hasn't told me anything.*" In response, he said, "*The Lord will speak to you, but don't tell anyone about this. So, let us pray.*" Then I thought within myself, I'm not going to pray. I did not believe that God had told him that. I thought since his first wife was sick for so long that he was lusting.

How wrong I was!

God had spoken to him even before his first wife had died. He said the Lord told him to marry Sister Fields, and take care of her. So, after he asked me for an answer, I told him that I had not heard a word from the Lord. So, after about three weeks, he called my daughter Bernice, and asked her could he come over to her house for dinner next Thursday. Oh!, she was happy, and agreed for him to come over for dinner. When she got off the phone, she said to me, "*Mother that was Pastor and he wants to come over for dinner next Thursday"*, which was my day off.

I was working with my Mother and two brothers, and they all three shared the rent. But my job was to strip the bottom of chairs and re-cover them again. My hands were bruised and cut, but I thank God for the job because I had no other income at that time. Not knowing that our God had spoken to the man of God. What a mighty God we serve!

My daughter asked me to help her with dinner next Thursday. After dinner, my daughter cleared the table of the first course meal, and was making the desert. Then our Bishop said to Minister Evans and Bernice, "*The reason I asked you about coming to dinner is because I had something to say to you all. I plainly asked her not to say anything to anyone about what I asked of her. I know she didn't say anything because I asked her not to. But the Lord had shown me that she would be my next wife*".

When he spoke those words, my son-in-law and my daughter Bernice began to praise God mightily while I looked at him with a disgusting look. Of course, this was a very strange situation, but when they calmed down, our Bishop continued the conversation by saying, "*Elder Evan and Missionary Bernice Williams, let us all fast and pray for three days because I believe God will answer our prayers in guiding us on the right path*". So, the second day of the fast, I began to feel different, and I began to feel the presence of the Lord mightily in the Spirit and it began to take control of my mind. I asked the Lord, "*Why should I marry him?*", and the Lord replied, "*For the up building of My Kingdom*".

And the Lord began to speak to me, and said, "*If you don't marry him, then you will marry someone that could take you out of the Lord*". So, at the end of the fast, that afternoon, we had just finished our soup, and then the phone rang. It was Bishop Morris. My daughter answered the phone, and said, "*Yes sir, we made it*". Then, he asked to speak to me. I said, "*Hello!*". He said, "*Sister Fields, did the Lord say anything to you?*" I said, "*You know what Bishop, I'll go through with it, but I don't love you*". He replied, "*I know you don't, but you will*". At the same time, the housekeeper was listening on the phone to the conversation. As soon as I agreed to marry Bishop, he said, "*I'm so glad you agreed, darling I couldn't live without you because the Lord told me to marry you, and take care of you*". Bishop asked, "*When can I pick you up and get the things you need?*" I replied, "*Whenever you can*".

The following week, he came and took me shopping. He brought my ring and a couple of outfits to wear. I began to feel happy about my upcoming marriage. Then that Friday night when I was sitting in the choir stand, I felt coldness in the church but I didn't know why. As I began to clap my hands, and the sister sitting next to me grabbed my left hand. She snatched my ring, and slung my hand back and told me, "*So, you going through with it, huh!*" It scared me so bad. Then, the Spirit came to me, and made me realize why it was cold in here.

Soon after the service was dismissed, I headed straight for the door without speaking to anyone. I was just a few steps from the bus stop when I heard someone calling my name, "*Sister Fields!*" Lo, and behold, it was Bishop Morris. He told me he was going to drive me home. I told him, "*No sir! Bishop, I can catch the bus*". He said to me, "*Wait until I lock the doors of the church*". So, I waited, and he drove me to my sister Marie house. And when he turned the corner on 39th & Oakland Boulevard, I went inside of the house and got my suitcase because I was leaving the city. Mind you, I didn't have money, but I made a phone call to Pastor Dickson not knowing that she was in love with Bishop, too. I told her I wanted to go to Gary, Indiana to my sister's house. She said, "*Get a cab and come to my house*".

When I made it to her house, she was in the bedroom combing her hair and I said to her, "*Pastor Dickson, I'm not going to marry Bishop Morris*". She said to me, "*No, you don't need to. If you do, it will tear up his church*". So, she gave me money to pay the cab driver. He took me to 63rd & King Drive to the bus station. I boarded a bus and went to Gary, Indiana to my sister's house Louise. I was there only a few days when I began to feel uncomfortable in my spirit. So, I called Pastor Rebecca Williams and she was so happy to have me come over to her church.

Pastor Williams had an apartment over the church. Everyday she would leave to go to work. But before she would leave for work, she would leave cereal, milk, soup and crackers on the counter. So, the day before I came off the fast, she came home and said to me, "*Sister Fields, you haven't eaten anything yet?*" I replied, "*No ma'am!*" She said, "*You need to come off that hunger strike, and go marry my Bishop*". I said to myself, "*I'm not talking to her any more*". But the day, I was ending the fast, it was around 2:45p.m. I got on my knees in front of the couch. I said, "Lord have mercy on me", and I began to cry. I said, "*Lord show me what to do*". The Lord said to me, "*You coward you! You would have married Bishop, but you were afraid of what people would say*". Then I began to repent and say, "*Lord, forgive me, I will do it*".

After I said that, I went to the kitchen and poured a glass of milk, and opened a can of soup. But before I finished, the phone rang. It was my sister Marie. I picked up the phone, and she said to me, "*Tina, why did you run off and didn't tell nobody where you were?*" And she said, "*Let me tell you one thing. All you Pentecostal niggas fooled around, and can give my Mother a heart attack. I will have all of you in the paper*". Then she said, "*I want to ask you one question. Are you going to marry my brother Morris?*" And I said, "*I'm coming home. The Lord told me what to do*", and she hung up the phone. On my way back to the kitchen, I heard a voice, and it was Bishop Morris. He said, "*Why did you run away?*", and I said, "*Bishop, I didn't want to tear up the church*". He said to me, "*It was already torn up*". But I want to ask you one question, "*Can I come and pick you up and take you home?*" And I said, "*Yes sir!*"

It was a service night downstairs when Pastor Rebecca returned home from work. I told her that

Bishop was coming over, and after service, he will drive me back to Chicago.

Life married to Bishop was what I truly needed to fulfill the purpose God called us to. Our experiences together will always be with me. More about my life with Bishop Morris is written further in the pages of this book.

Chapter II: Her Love
"Down Through The Years"

Introduction to her teachings . . . .

Some people make themselves a spiritual leader. But in order for one to become a good spiritual leader, one must be a faithful servant under one leader before they can be promoted or exalted by that leader you are under. God lets them know when it is the right time because in the Word of the Lord, God always spoke to the leader about their ministers who were under them, and that minister to lay hands on you, and to promote you by giving you some of their honor. God told Moses to openly lay hands on Joshua in front of the congregation. Therefore, public ordination is so important. There must be a laying on of the hands in order to release spiritual authority and spiritual discipline. There is also an impartation of wisdom.

Wisdom is the key to a fruitful and spiritual life.

Apostle Christine Morris

The Church And Its Purpose

It has been said that the most important aspect in the life of a new believer is the attendance of the church. At church, you will receive instruction and exhortation as to how to live a life full of the Holy Spirit. You will grow up and increase or decrease depending on your attendance to church. Every service is planned with you in mind. Church will help you strengthen your mind, will power and emotions to remain firm in the Lord.

The Purpose of the Church

Matthew 28:19-20, "*Therefore go make disciples of all nations, baptizing them in the name of the Father and of the Son, and of the Holy Spirit, and teaching them to obey everything I have commanded you. And surely I am with you always, to the end of the age.*" (Emphasis added)

1. To make disciples

2. Change lives

3. To keep His Word

The Need for Administration in the Church

I Corinthians 12:1-12

This passage of scripture is the clearest single group of scriptures concerning the need of administration in the local church. Paul tells the Corinthian church that everyone in the body of Christ has gifts and a place of function; but the Holy Spirit also has explicit instructions without that, some form of structure or guidance, members of the body would have difficulty identifying their own gift and their proper function and finding their place. (I Corinthians 12:15-17)

There is a tremendous need for everyone to work together and this is why we need administration applied to the body. Moses took personal responsibility, then later delegated it to several men who caused the multitude of Israel to find rest (Exodus 18:13-26)

It is interesting to note that whenever there is a properly structured administration, the people find rest. The job of administration in the church is to delegate responsibility to proper individuals so that no one person is <u>overworked</u>.

Administration has been defined as, "*Coordinating Co-Equal Ministries*".

The Father took the initiative and the planning, and Jesus, through the power of the Holy Spirit, actually carried out the plan of the creation (Genesis 1). Although co-equal in relationship, the Father exercised seniority of command because of His function as initiator and planner (Colossians 1:16). In much, the same way, the Pastor is the Senior Administrator of the church, due to function. Although he/she does not have to physically carry out all the various tasks connected with the church, he/she is still the initiator and the overall planner of all the areas of the church.

The Job Description of the Business Administrator

- he/she answers to the president of the corporation
- submit to the Pastor
- submit to the goals of the church
- commit to the goals of the church
- endue with the Holy Spirit, and love and have concern for the people

- o prioritize – understand what is important and what is "*urgent*"

The Art of Getting Things Done

The art of getting things done assumes an understanding that important things come first:

- o Do the most important things first, even if it is difficult
- o Plan your week so that everything does not have to be done the following week
- o Make needed improvements before irritations become complaints

Conclusion

It is suggested that we pray the prayer that Elisha prayed when he asked God for a double portion of Elijah's spirit (II Kings 2:9-10)

- o Know your leader; get his/her spirit. Know his/her heartbeat

Remember Colossians 4:6,
"*Let your speech [be] always with grace, seasoned with salt; that ye may know how ye ought to answer every man.*"

Prayer and Fasting

Prayer is fellowshipping with the Lord of the Father – a vital personal contact with God who is more than enough. We are to be in constant communion with the Lord because I Peter 3:12 says, *"For the eyes of the Lord are upon the righteous,..."* – those who are upright and in the right standing with the Lord – and His ears are attentive and open to their prayer.

Prayer is not to be a religious form with no power. It is to be effective and accurate and bring results. God watches over His Word to perform it (Jeremiah. 1:12)

Prayer that brings results must be based on God's Word.

Proverbs 15:8
Colossians 1:9-13
John 15:8

We must pray for all men (1 Timothy 2:1)

If not, we sin everywhere!

Why Should We Fast?

To minister unto the Lord

To increase our faith (Matthew 17:19-20) "... *nothing should be impossible unto you.*"

To see the vision

Some people have visions of heaven and glory and angels, and it greatly increases their faith. "... *I will cause you to ride upon high places of the earth ...*" (Isaiah. 58:14)

To give ourselves to the Lord (I Corinthians. 7:5)

To work in the Spirit (Romans. 8:1-13)

The Bible teaches us there is a continued conflict between the flesh and the Spirit, and between our natural desire and the Spirit of the Lord. Much of the old man is still alive. If you fast two or three days, you will gain the victory over the flesh. Denial means not eating twelve midnight until noon, or from three o'clock to six o'clock, and totally abstain from food. Three days without food or water is a complete fast (72 hours).

Fasting brings more faith in the Word of God (Mark 11:23-24).

Responsibility of a Good Pastor

Pastors are to feed, protect and guide God's people, and also be a good Shepherd of God's Flock

God's people in the New Testament times are Pastors, and in the Old Testament times Shepherds. The purpose is to admonish, instruct and direct recipients in their personal lives and duties.

Pastors are called by God, and chosen by Him to care and organize the church as well as feed the flock of God.

A Pastor is called by God to guard the Christian Faith and to Appoint Qualified Officials to Conduct Proper Worship, and to maintain Discipline, both personally and in the Churches.

A Pastor gives Instructions in the work of the church: To guard against the False Doctrines and Unholy Living.

A Pastor teaches that the Morals and Purity of Christians should be maintained. Also, a New Pastor should abide by Paul's Writings to Young Pastors (Timothy and Titus)

In I Timothy 6:20, Paul charges the Young Pastor to maintain the Faith and to be Fruitful to the Church.

Paul told Timothy to guard what was committed to his trust. This Declaration is the Heart of the Pastorship, all this is to be done by the Indwelling Power of the Holy Ghost.

Pastors are to avoid Hearsay, and Hold to Sound doctrine and Maintain Purity of Life, and we must be Good shepherds for Christ's Sake. (St. John 10) – Shepherds of Leaders of the Church.

Effective Leadership

From Envision to Vision
- *"Write the vision and make it plain"* – Habakkuk 2:2

What you say and see, you can have – Mark 11:23-24

Dare to Plan:
- Pray
- Strategize
- Organize and not Agonize

Plan smart, you won't have to work hard!

Pick people who love God and you.

Set the goals:
- People who will buy into your vision and ministry

Work SMART:
- S – Specific

- M – Measurable
- A – Attainable
- R – Realistic
- T – Time related ministry

Not HARD:
- H – Hindrance
- A – Attested
- R – Religious
- D – Doings

Pray about it. Check with the scriptures
- Is it against His Word?

Go after your Vision and Dream – Don't Let Go!

You can do it!

Understanding Pastoral Attacks through Relationships

It is important to know and understand when an attack is being made upon a Pastor. It is not good because their personal identity and faith is under siege. An attack on a Pastor is an attack on his or her total existence.

There are signs which indicate an attack on a Pastor. Understand, there are many conflicts among churches today. But thank God for the Holy Ghost! Acts 15th Chapter gives us how to handle conflict among Pastors and Leadership which usually affect all or some of the congregation. There are warning signs that tells us conflict is brewing in the church. Good communication is the key to good relationships. Understand that it is not good to receive a member from a Fellowshipping Church before communicating with his/her former Pastor. We must be aware that Satan can use Church Members to bring conflict and reproach on another Leader. Satan has many devices he uses just to destroy the love of God that we have for the Kingdom of God as One Body.

We are to use the Bible as the basis of our teachings, and that is, "*let us pray for one another*". The Pastors should do all in their power to enable the congregation to be strong in the Lord, so that the church will be all that God intended for it to be.

So let us pray for all Missions to be accomplished in the work of the Lord, and for this is SERIOUS business. "*(For the weapons of our warfare [are] not carnal, but mighty through God to the pulling down of strong holds;)*" (II Corinthians 10:4)

Prayer is very essential.

God's people need us. The Church should be available for Spiritual Guidance, Counsel and assistance in Visitation.

We must teach the congregation through our conduct, and our life to love, to respect and to cooperate with the church. "*The blessings of the Lord, it maketh rich, and he add no sorrow with it.*" (Proverbs 10:22)

Let us love one another with a pure love (Proverbs 10:12).

Ministry and the Marketplace: Strategic Partnership

This will tell us how Saul and Samuel partnered together to lead God's people.

Samuel took the initiative and anointed Saul for the role he was to fulfill (I Samuel 10:1). Samuel did not feel competition or envy against this new leader. Samuel knew that both would serve as leaders among God's people. As complimentary partners, we are not here to compete with each other, but to complete each other.

Now Saul was doing the very thing Samuel had been gifted to do. Samuel didn't resist helping Saul to develop into the spiritual leader that God called him to be. Samuel encouraged Saul to use his spiritual gifts (I Samuel 10:10-13). Samuel helped Saul to revive a new heart for serving God's people.

The scripture provides a miraculous picture of how Pastors and business leaders can partner together to fulfill a God-given vision. First, Samuel shows how God uses Samuel, the Priest Ministry Leader, and Saul, the King Marketplace Leader. Samuel feels secure and is able to fulfill his role as a spiritual leader to this big strong, tall King Saul. Samuel does not envy Saul's role. Therefore, the devil could not cause Samuel to be diverted from his work in Saul's life. Saul could've been an intimidating leader (I Samuel 9:2). This denotes that the following partnerships of these two could come together to fulfill God's plan.

The Truth about the Prophet and the Prophetess

Samuel had a three-fold anointing. Samuel was a prophet, priest and judge. He possessed these three anointings and successfully communicated them to others through life impartation. As a prophet of God, he was able to be a divine messenger inspired and called by God.

Here are four descriptions of a prophet/prophetess:

1. Prophets/Prophetess declares God's Will (Ezra 5:2)

2. Prophets/Prophetess were described as God's servant (Zechariah 1:6)
3. Prophets/Prophetess are watchmen (Ezekiel 3:17)
4. Prophets/Prophetess are holy men/women of God (2 Peter 1:21)

In the New Testament, prophets were cited as a noble example of patient in the face of suffering (James 5:10). Another word for prophet is "*seer*". A prophetess is God's mouth piece, to speak for God. Sometimes the word God in their mouths is not always good news as it was with Huldah (2 Kings 22:13-20). Anna was a prophetess (Luke 2:36-38), and she never left the temple after the death of her husband.

God is moving again by His Spirit, and He is anointing and appointing Apostles, Prophets and Prophetess. During the Protestant Movement in the 1500's, it brought a restoration of, . . . the doctrine of dead works (Hebrews 6:1-2). This was the foundation of repentance from the acts that lead to death and of the faith in God. Instruction of Baptism, the laying on of the hands, the resurrection of the dead, and the eternal judgment, . . . if God permits us, we will do it.

The Picture of a Prophet: The Acceptance and Rejection

1. He is a Seer who comes to Lead the Blind. The Prophet is God's Detective;

He's Sweet I Know

2. Seeking the Lost Treasure. The Prophet of God is Measured of his Unpopularity. Compromise is not known to him;

3. He has no Price Tags;

4. He Marches to Another Drummer;

5. He Breathes the Purified Air of Inspiration;

6. He Lives in the Heights of God and Comes into the Valley with the Lord;

7. He Shares some of the Foreknowledge of God, and is aware of Impending Judgment;

8. He Lives in Splendid Isolation;

9. He is Forthright and Outright, but He claims no Birthright;

10. A Prophet comes to set up that which is upset. His work is to call into line those who are out of line;

11. A Prophet is Excommunicated while Alive and Exhalted when Dead;

12. He is Dishonored while Living and honored when Dead;

13. He is a SchoolMaster to bring us to Christ, but few make the Grade in his Class;

14. He is Friendless while Living and Famous when Dead;

15. He eats the Daily Bread of Affliction while he ministers, but He Feeds the Bread of Life to those Who Listens;

16. He walks before Men for days, but has walked before God for years;

17. He Announces, Pronounces and Denounces;

18. He has a Heart like a Volcano and his words are as Fire;

19. God Talks to him about Men; and

20. He talks to Men about God.

The Apostle and the Apostleship

The Apostle is the first gift of the church.

Paul defended the Apostleship. The word Apostle means one sent under Commission, and refers to the Twelve Apostles and Paul. These men had a special commission with the New Testament Prophets to Lay the Foundation of the Church.

One of the qualifications for being an Apostle was a personal experience of seeing the Resurrected Christ. (Acts 1:21-22, Acts 3:15, Acts 5:32, Acts 10:39-43) The Apostles were given the Ability to Perform Special Signs and Wonders to attest what they preached. (Hebrews 2:4, 2 Corinthians 12:12)

In Corinthians, Paul worked many miracles because Corinth was a difficult City to Minister. (Acts 18:1-7)

The Apostolic Governing Churches

The restoration of the Church and its Ministries:

- Characteristic of a governing church

- Take responsibility to keep a spiritually climate conducive

- Essential principles in building leadership

- Leadership must build according to the present day divine patterns

- Leadership must build with a future in view

- Leadership must have spirituality to build

- Leadership must gather necessary resources to build

- Leadership develop Apostolic wisdom to manage and arrange what had been built

There are three major concepts of building church principles: love, joy and peace with the guiding of the Holy Ghost. These concepts influence our actions.

The Beast and His Bride

Who is the beast? The beast is the anti-Christ. The bride is Babylon. The name of the anti-Christ bride is "*Babylon the great*". Some people ask why is a bride named of that city. This is not unusual because it is in the scripture. (Revelation 17:5)

"*Mystery Babylon the Great*" of anti-Christ; this is not a literal city. But a system of religious and apostate. Why?, . . . because of its inhabitants and not the city itself. "*As the church, the firstborn of Christ is the regenerated followers of Christ*". Revelation 21:9 states: "*Come hither, I will shew thee the bride, the lamb's wife.*" Instead of showing him a woman, he showed him a city, the "*Holy Jerusalem*". Descending out of heaven from God, here we see a city which is called a bride. *"Mystery of Babylon"*, the Great, the bride of anti-Christ, will be composed of followers of all False Religions.

Genesis 2:10 refers to a river flowing through the Garden of Eden. Its water is divided into the four branched unknown today.

> The first is Pison, which flowed around the center land of Havilah, where gold is found. The gold of the land is exceptionally pure, Aromatic resin onyx stones are also found there.
>
> The second is Gihon, which flowed around the entire land of Ethiopia.
>
> The third was Hiddekel, which goeth toward the east of Assyria.
>
> The fourth is Euphrates.

The River that flowed into the Garden of Eden was divided. Satan doubtless chose the site of Babylon as his headquarters from which *"Sally Forth"* attempted Adam and Eve. It was doubtless here that the Antediluvian Apostasy had its source that ended in the flood. To this Centre, the forces of evil gravitated after the flood, and Babel was the result of this origin of nations. The nations were not scattered abroad over the earth until Satan had implanted in them the virus of a doctrine that had been the source of every false religion. This was beginning with Adam and Eve in the Garden of Eden. The Lord forbade them to eat the forbidden fruit. Satan spread this virus through disobedience. Eve disobeyed by listening to the deceiver Satan. She saw it was good for food and to be desired. Satan had told her it would make one wise and you shall be as gods. Now, the virus of Satan is in full force.

God says that it is not good for man to be alone. I will make him a companion who will help him. So, the Lord God caused Adam to fall in a deep sleep. He took one of Adam's ribs and closed up the place. Then the Lord God made a woman from the rib and brought her to Adam. At least Adam proclaimed she was part of my flesh and she will be called woman. Why? . . . because she was taken out of man. This explains why a man should leave his father and mother, and be joined to his wife. The two are united into one. Although Adam and his wife were both naked, they were not ashamed. Why were they not ashamed? . . . because they were innocent. They were created in an innocent state just like God. But when the time came, Satan deceived the people as he did Eve in the garden, and that was to make a great name for them to be like God.

The Anti-Christ Coming Out of Assyria

(Genesis 10:8-10) Cush begat Nimrod; he began to be a mighty one in the earth. Nimrod was a mighty hunter before the Lord. And the beginning of his kingdom was Babel.

Genesis 11:4, *"Let us build us city and a tower, whose top may reach unto heaven."*

Understand that there is an ancient kingdom between the Tigris and Euphrates River which became the dominant power in the ancient world about 900 to 700 B.C. The Assyrians was aggressive and war like people who were known for their cruelty in warfare often cutting off their victim heads and hands, and putting them on stakes as Gods to humiliate the people. Haddam Hussein did this, too. And Bin-Laden will be back, too for this cruel and pagan act. The Old Testament Prophets commanded them. Isaiah 10:5, Ezekiel 16:28, Hosea 8:9. The region which was developed into Assyria was originally settled by the greater Nimrod, the descendant of Noah (Genesis 10:18-12). The first name for Assyria was Asshur, after a son of Shem (Genesis 10:11). So, the King Shalmaneser invaded Judah (II King 18:13).

So, later about 722 B.C., the King Shalmaneser overthrew the northern kingdom, which are the tribes of Israel enslaved many of its inhabitants and resettled the region with foreigners (II Kings 18:9-11, Ezra 4:2). Also Asshur, Minlueh is the capital of Assyria. On the Tigris River, God's message of judgment by Jonah 3:3, founded by Asshur, the son of Shem Ninleh, reached the height of wealth and splendor in Jonah's time.

Because Satan has united Rome and Babylon as one, this is why the Pope is coming out of Rome, and now has made his way to the greatest country, the Unites States of America. This country is going to be in great persecution between Catholicism and the Apostolic Movement.

Practical Nuggets of Wisdom

Our Christian Relationship

"Love not the world, neither the things that are in the world. If any man love the world, the love of the Father is not in him. For all that is in the world, lust of the flesh, and the lust of the eyes, and the pride of life, is not of the Father, but is of the world."
(I John 2:15-16)

Our Christian relationship to the world is not to love the world. This means that in this vast society, Satan has promoted the indifference of God. Satan's system of this day and age consists of evil immorality and sinful pleasures of the world. This also refers to the spirit of rebellion against God and His Revelation that exists within all human traits and characteristics. Satan uses the world's ideas, morals, mental and psychological tactics through our government and economic systems, cultures, education, science, art, medicine, music and entertainment, sports and the mass media to distract God's people from living and fulfilling our lives with Him. Satan has used all these things that are in the world to oppose God's Word, His people and His Righteous standards (Matthew 16:26).

For example, Satan will use the medical industry to promote the killing of unborn babies, the agriculture that produce life, . . . displaying drugs such as alcohol and narcotics as a way to promote ungodly values and lowering humanistic standards, and kinds of entertainment to destroy the Godly fear and reverence. But we, as Believers in Christ, must be aware and know that behind all human characteristics that there is a spirit and power that moves against God and His Word. Also, we must know and understand that this world includes man-made religious systems, and they all are unbiblical, worldly and lukewarm Christian organizations and churches.

If we continue to love the world with our flesh, then it will defy our fellowship with God and lead us to spiritual destruction.

Addiction

"Don't give up on yourself because God will never give up on you." (II Peter 3:9, Judges 1:24)

People are getting hooked on so many things. Addictions start with a decision that leads to a series of steps like a habit. There are habits you cannot break without God's supernatural help. One generation is called the "*hooked on generation*". Millions of people are hooked on alcohol, and others are hooked on sex and are destroying themselves and others. The HIV/Aids epidemic is threatening to exterminate an entire generation.

"Now unto him that is able to keep you from falling." (Jude 24a)

Why do people get hooked? Well, there are many reasons why people become addicted to bad habits: (1) peer pressure, and (2) a search to fill a personal emptiness, . . . but Isaiah 55:1 says, *"Ho, every one that thirsteth, come ye to the waters, and he that hath no money; come ye, buy, and eat; yea, come, buy wine and milk without money and without price."*

St. John 4:14 says, *"But whosoever drinketh of the water that I shall give him shall never thirst; but the water that I shall give him shall be in him a well of water springing up into everlasting life."*

Hooked on Alcohol

Alcoholism in America was estimated around ten (10) million alcoholics, with only three percent on skid row. This bad habit has caused many health problems, heart disease and cancer. But remember that the Word of God says in Matthew 1:21, *"And she shall bring forth a son, and thou shalt call his name JE-SUS: for he shall save his people from their sins"*. (see Acts 10:38-48)

Hooked on Nicotine

Some people are hooked on what suppose to be the most harmless drug, . . . cigarettes. However, the addiction habit of smoking can be the hardest of all to break because smoking provides a slight high of nicotine and causes the nervousness that must be repeated frequently. Smokers who get hooked stand in danger of lung cancer and heart disease, but not realizing the real tragedy of smoking is that it kills its victims slowly.

Habits are something you must fight yourself, and with God's help you can win any battle if you surrender totally to God. Turn your body, soul and mind completely over to God. Say to yourself what Paul wrote in Philippians 4:13 *"I can do all things through Christ which strengtheneth me."* (Philippians 1:6)

Hooked on Marijuana

Some people are addicted to marijuana, the most common drug used in America today. It is particularly known as *"pot"*, *"weed"* or *"grass"*. Marijuana comes from the flowery top and leaves of the Indian plant. After the plant is cut, the leaves and flowers are dried and crushed, and then smoked in a hand-rolled cigarette called a *"joint"* which is very dangerous. People underestimate its addiction power. If we all must be addicted, let him or her be addicted to the work of Christ (I Corinthians 16:13-16)[1]

Hooked on Cocaine

Some people are addicted to cocaine which is especially dangerous, and it was once called the *"rich man's drug"*. *"Coke"* is now available to everyone, and it is especially prominent among twenty and thirty year olds. Cocaine is a powerful drug, and it raises the blood pressure and increases the rate of respiration and causes irregular heart beats. Not only will it turn you on, but it will turn you off permanently.

Remember what the Word of God says in Romans 6:23, *"For the wages of sin is death: but the gift of God is eternal life through Jesus Christ our Lord."*

Hooked on LSD

Some people are addicted to L.S.D. popularly known as *"Angel Dust"*, and it will put you in the dust for good. But Jesus said in St. John 10:10b, *"I am come that they might have life and that they might have it more abundantly"*. L.S.D., S.T.P. and P.C.P., and supposedly *"glue"* has a tragic affect which leads you

---

[1] Because this book was originally written early on, more drugs and terms have been changed over the years. Now, instead of smoking joints, some Marijuana smokers are rolling blunts (tobacco leaf). They are smoking Cush, Hydro, Leaf, etc.

from one drug to another until you are hooked for life. But Jesus can bring you out if you ask Him. The Bible says in St. Luke 11:9-10 says, *"And I say unto you, Ask, and it shall be given you; seek, and ye shall find; knock, and it shall be opened unto you. For every one that asketh receiveth; and he that seeketh findeth; and to him that knocketh it shall be opened."*

Getting unhooked, the Word of God says that it is *"Quick and powerful and sharper than any two-edged sword, piercing even to the dividing asunder of soul and spirit, and of the joints and marrow, and is a discerner of the thoughts and intents of the heart."* (Hebrews 4:12). God has blessed us because we know that the only way for anyone to get *"unhooked"* from anything is through the Blood of Jesus Christ (Acts 4:12, Philippians 4:13, John 1:9). With God, no matter what habits you are struggling with, our God is able (Jude 24). Understand, you can overcome it by yielding your all to God.

We all understand and realize that getting addicted starts with a series of steps, therefore, getting *"unhooked"* works the same way. First, you must face the serious consequences of addiction and then decide that you want to quit. Of course, it will take every effort, but you can do it. Secondly, you must admit to yourself that you are hooked, and then stop making excuses, and confess to God your addiction. You will have to start by admitting it to yourself that no one overcomes without confessing it. The Bible says in I John 1:9, *"If we confess our sins, he is faithful and just to forgive us our sins, and to cleanse us from all unrighteousness."*

He's Sweet I Know

With any bad habit, you must admit your weakness and be determined to do something about it. One thing you must do, and that is to hate your habit. But the only way you can hate sin or evil is to have God because He hates all evil. David said, "*Order my steps in thy word: and let not any iniquity have dominion over me.*" (Psalm 119:133), . . . and "*I hate vain thoughts: but thy law do I love. Thou art my hiding place and my shield: I hope in thy word. Depart from me, ye evildoers: for I will keep the commandments of my God.*" (Psalm 119:113-115).

As I said before, . . . "*Don't give up on yourself because God will not give up on you*".

Chapter III: Her Legacy
"He's Sweet I Know"

He's Sweet I Know

The Church History: First Pentecostal

Bishop James Morris was a member of the Zion Hill Baptist Church where he served as an Usher and Deacon. On November 23, 1929, he was sanctified and filled with the Holy Ghost at All Nations Pentecostal Church. His call to the ministry became a reality in 1935 when the late Mother Lucy Smith ordained him. He was faithful to his spiritual calling, and was a living testimony to the words of the scripture, "... *Men ought to always pray and not faint*" (Luke 18:1). The growth of the church, in which Pastor Morris served, resulted from his trust in the Lord, and his loving solicitude for the spiritual welfare of his flock. We were told in the early days that Mother Morris held services in the living room, and later in the basement of their home. After which, the Lord gave her a 40 day and 40 night revival, and many souls were saved.

The Lord blessed Elder Morris' perseverance by inspiring him to equip the church with chairs and pews, and to hold prayer services. In 1940, he opened a church at 3143 South Cottage Grove. As the congregation grew, he moved the church to 3202 South Cottage Grove under the leadership of the late Bishop J.D. Smith of Church of God Mission Society. The Lord blessed His servant's humbleness by favoring young people to join the church, and they began to sing to the Lord.

In 1943, Pastor Morris adhered to the Will of God, with many churches under his leadership, ordained many pastors, deacons, missionaries and evangelists. Through all his countless hardships and many experiences, Bishop Morris had manifested his abiding love for the people of God.

In 1947, Bishop Morris saw a church at 1517-19 West Hastings, and prayed that the Lord would provide both a spiritual and financial blessing for the purchase and ownership of this church. It was indeed a crowning glory to his many achievements that the mortgage on this church was paid off in three years. We had all summed it up with Bishop's favorite song, *"All That I Need Is In Jesus"*, and his scriptural passage, *"Fear Not Little Flock"*.

The Lord laid our beloved Bishop Morris home to rest on January 15, 1981 from his labor, and Mother Ardella Morris had preceded him in death.

He's Sweet I Know

In February 1985, the Lord had blessed us to move into our new location, 5146 South Ashland Avenue.

1990: Our First Church Challenge

For ten months, we went through a trying time about the building because it was time for us to pay it off. Our five years were up. We were so sure we had seven years. But at the end of five years, the bank got in touch with me and said we had to pay the building off which cost one hundred and fifty thousand dollars. God had blessed us to pay seventy-four or seventy-six thousand dollars from 1985 to the first part of 1990. I thanked God for His many blessings to First Pentecostal! We did not have the money that we needed so we asked the bank to refinance the building in which they agreed to do. Thank God! But in doing so, they came up with a bill, a tax bill, with the amount of nine thousand dollars.

From the nineteen eighty-five taxes, we had a big problem, and I mean a BIG problem. But God worked in our favor. God was our lawyer because the lawyer we had did not do right in the beginning because it should have been made clear that when we bought the building that because of our non-profit status, we were tax exempt.

So, on October 3, 1990, we went downtown for the closing, Thank God! The closing date was October 3, 1990 at 2:30 p.m. at 111 West Washington Street, 3rd floor. It was myself, Pastor Christine Morris, Evangelist Bernice Williams - Vice President and

Business Administrator, Minister John C. Kimble - Assistant Pastor, Elder Thomas Parker - Trustee, Elder Walter Moore – Elder's Board Chairman, Evangelist Josephine Taylor – Secretary, Evangelist Ann Bell – Treasurer and Deacon Willie McGee – Deacon Board Chairman. The Title & Trust had each of us sign the refinance papers, and they presented us with a check for First Pentecostal Church in the amount we had asked for. The Title & Trust company took out four hundred dollars. But God blessed us to have two thousand dollars left in our escrow account.

I thank God because in the beginning, it looked like we were going to be defeated. At one point, it looked like we really had no choice but to pay the taxes. The bank Secretary said to me, "*Ms. Morris, you know you could loose your building. Mike, your lawyer, was saying you have to pay the nine thousand dollars in taxes*". I truly thank and praise God because all of our good days had out-weighed our bad days.

Thanks be unto God who giveth us the victory! We came out as the winner at the finish line.

He's Sweet I Know

My Family

Mother Henrietta Williams

My loving mother, Henrietta Williams was the greatest mother a daughter could ever have. We all called her Momma, but her husband called her "*Sweet*". My mother had five girls, and she would have given her life if she could. My mother and I really loved each other. Before God saved us, we had a mother-daughter love and it was great. We lived as though we loved each other. My mother was there when no one was there.

My Mother often talked about how she was raised up at an early age. I had always felt bad because she was brought up without a mother. But I thank God that He took care of my mother. I can truly say, "*Thank You Lord*", for keeping my Mother and her baby sister A.P. Clark. God had blessed her with four children; one son and three daughters.

My Mother was a great woman of God who served faithfully as a Mother in First Pentecostal, and taught wisdom as a dedicated and committed Sunday School Teacher until the Lord took her home.

Believe me when I say that there is no love like my mother's love because it is real.

Bernice and her Children

The Lord has blessed me with such a wonderful daughter, Bernice. I had always known that the Lord was upon her life. God has blessed her and I. Personally I believe that God wants to do more in her life and with her life. My prayer is that my daughter, Bernice, will forever walk with the Lord.

She truly loves her four children; her two boys and her two girls. My oldest grandson is Reggie, and I believe God had used him in a special way. I had prayed to God to use him before he was even born, and I asked the Lord to save him at an early age. Karen is the second oldest child and she was a very sweet and wise child. She had always talked and acted like she had been around for a long time and she was only seven years old. I had prayed to the Lord that God would save her at an early age, too. Third in line was Christopher who was so loving, but a strange child.

He's Sweet I Know

Ever since he was a baby, he had been trying to praise God in his own little way. Someday, I had believed that he would preach, and live for the Lord every step of the way. And last, but not least, my baby girl Marcie. As much as Marcie loved her grandmother, she really had a special love for her grandfather.

My grandchildren have always had a wonderful mother and a caring father. I knew that the Lord had His hand upon their lives. Sometimes I had felt that I wasn't doing enough to care for them, but God knew my heart's desire.

I thank God for them, and I truly love my family with all my heart.

Speak The Truth Fellowship

In 2000, God had given me a vision and a mission of the Speak The Truth Fellowship to Help Build Up, Strengthen, Encourage and Support pastors with their church visions as they labor in the vineyard.

Our purpose was to meet at a fellowshipping pastors' church and raise funds for their ministry. We held these services every second Monday of each month. We had asked each participating member to contribute to the offering that was being raised for that particular ministry with whom we fellowshipped.

Each participating member was not obligated to make every service. We had understood as a Pastor that there were other obligations. However, if a Pastor was not able to attend a service, they were encouraged to show their support by sending their contribution and sending a representative from their ministry.

We had raised 2 offerings: one for the Fellowshipping Church and one for the Speaker. Each Pastor was responsible for coordinating their programs and services. By doing so, we had asked the Pastor to prayerfully select service participants that can flow in the Spirit of God. We had always wanted to encourage, inspire and motivate the people of God to exercise their gifts.

We scheduled meetings for all members so that everyone in the fellowship could be updated on the current and upcoming events. We also mailed the information in a timely manner.

As a member, we asked that every fellowshipping church would raise an offering on every fifth Sunday for the fellowship. That money went towards the three-day Speak The Truth Fellowship Conference that was held every year in May.

I thank God for the Speak the Truth Fellowship. God blessed us to be a blessing to so many churches in Chicago and in several other states.

To God be the Glory for the things He has done!

The Passing of the Torch

I love Jesus Christ today because He had put on my heart to crown my daughter, Co-Pastor Bernice Williams, as the Pastor of this great church, First Pentecostal Church of God, Inc. The Lord had me to do this while I was closed in my right mind because I was not able to do all the things that I would like to do. There was no greater person that I knew than my own daughter, Bernice because she was saved and sanctified in the same year that the Lord had saved and sanctified me and filled me with the Holy Ghost and called me into the ministry. At the same time, I did not understand it at that time. But the co-founder, Mother Ardella Morris said that God has done a great thing in my daughter's life. What a blessing it was to know such a woman of God like that. I was the one she taught how to serve the Lord in real true holiness, and now I have worked before my only daughter, the Co-Pastor and Assistant to the Apostleship. Praise the Lord!

I have bestowed all my blessings upon her because I knew she was the future of this church. She knows what it will be like because she walked closely with me in ministry as my co-pastor. I had understood that the future was evolving so quickly and that it would take a perceptive leader to keep abreast with the changes and work in an apostolic strategy to be effective. One thing for certain, those who know Him and walk with Him are qualified to lead this generation. With God's guidance and grace, our pastor will be able to lead this generation.

Although I knew that the heat of the battle is intensifying, the demonic attack on the Christian church was getting more and more pronounced. But one must understand that God is not a weak God. He is strong. Therefore, He is sent forth and raised up a leader that is more bold and courageous.

Our pastor is a pioneer and she possesses an inner energy of hope that helps those to press towards their future and destiny for their life. With her leadership, this generation will understand her vision and will not have fear of the unknown because they will grab hold to her heart and see her vision become a reality. Our pastor is a strong leader who will be able to stand in the midst of the storm and proclaim the victory in any spiritual warfare. Our pastor has learned how to build in the Spirit and effectively pull down the strongholds of the enemy.

Our Lord and Saviour Jesus Christ has made a shift in this leadership. Certainly, God has been mighty good to us in the Kingdom, especially towards the First Pentecostal Church of God, Inc.

I thank and Praise God because He has given us another good leader to continue the work of this ministry . . . Dr. Bernice Williams.

Reflections of My Life

I thank God for His goodness to me and His church. I am grateful that He called me to His service in 1957. God saved me and filled me with the Holy Ghost . . . Thank You Jesus! Truly God is good.

Down through the years, God has been real good to me. Before the Lord saved me, I was very sick because of the nature of sin and unconfessed sin in my life. God was calling me to holiness. But I did not believe that anyone was living right. I knew I was not living right and the people I was associated with was not living for God even though they were professing that they were. But I can feel the call of God every so often because from time to time, the Spirit of the Lord would speak to me. I will always remember telling God that I did not know why He wanted me to live right. And God said to me "*. . . because no one else is living right down there*". Oh, how blind was I! I was living wrong and doing wrong. Because I was wrong, Satan, had blinded my mind and my eyes. But thank God for the victory.

According to II Corinthians 4:3-4, . . . pride was in me and every evil deed was working in me because Satan had control of me. But when God spoke to me one morning, He spoke three times. And the last time He spoke, He said to me, "*How long will you live in your sin? You will die in your sin.*" I told the world that I cried with my whole heart unto God. "*Lord, save me. I want to be saved. Oh Glory!*" I cried not just a little while, but I cried until God saved me. When I came to myself, I was saying, "*Thank You Almighty God*". When I first began to pray, all I could hear was the deceiver saying, **"It's too late. You have been too bad, and you cannot go to all of those people that you have done wrong."** In response, I began to say, "*Oh God, I know that You created the Heavens and the Earth, and I know you can save me. You have all power in Your hand, . . . Thank You Jesus!*" And God did so. And that's why I am saved today, and it's been over fifty years ago. Praise God! This did not make me big, but I give God the glory for saving me because I know that God can, and God will save others.

I'm glad somebody prayed for me.

He's Sweet I Know

I went to church one Sunday morning, the First Pentecostal Church of God. My little daughter, Bernice was twelve or thirteen at the time. Nevertheless, we went to this church service, and my daughter said, "*Mom Dear, why are we going in this church?*" Inside of me said, . . . "*tell her we made it to this church*". And she said, "*. . . but this is a sanctified church*". And I said, "*. . . we won't be here long, come on.*" So, she and I went on upstairs into the sanctuary. The service had already begun. We sat there for a while. The choir was singing, but I could not understand why those choir members did not have any make-up on their faces. In my mind, I was saying to myself, I could not live like that. But while I was thinking on that, the choir began to sing a song called, "*Now Let Us Sing Until The Power of the Lord Come Down*". I did not know what they were saying or singing at that time because I was so busy finding fault. But all of a sudden, a little man got up at the pulpit and began to pray. But I said to my daughter, "*Let's go!*" So, we arose out of our seats and came down the aisle with our fingers raised. We went down the stairs and almost made it to the front door when we heard a voice saying to me, "*Lady!, Lady!*" I looked up the stairs and there stood a heavy-set lady still saying, "*Lady!, Lady!*", because she did not know my name. Before I said, "*Yes!*", she said the Pastor wants to see you. I said, "*Me!*", and she said, "*Yes!*" Before I could say anything, she said, "*He wants to pray for you.*" Thank You Jesus! I looked at my daughter, and I said, "*Come on, Bernice. It won't take long.*" See, when that lady said, "*. . . he wanted to pray for you*", I was afraid to go back in the church for prayer. Because growing up, we had heard so much about sanctified folks. I had been told that if they want to pray for you, then you should let them do it. Because if you refuse to take heed to them, then something bad could happen to you.

So, I went back upstairs into the sanctuary, and the Pastor, that little man that I saw when the choir was singing, said to me as I went down the aisles, "*Come on up here daughter.*" He was wiping his eyes when I went up there. Thanks be unto God! I saw him when he took his finger and put it over the top of a bottle of Olive Oil and put it on my neck. As he was praying for me, my eyes opened up. But when he brought his hand down from my neck and across my chest, a load fell from my shoulders, and it felt like I could fly. I was saying, "*Thank You Almighty God!*" Oh, I was crying because I felt good.

After I came down, I arose and went out again. While I was yet crying, we came to the bottom of the stairs and headed to go out onto the streets. I heard that same lady saying to me, "*Lady, what's your name?*", and I said, "*Christine Fields*". And she said, "*Where do you live?*", and I said, " . . . *in the projects, Apt. 906*". She asked, "*Do you have a phone?*", and I said, "*No!*" I didn't have a phone because we had just moved in the projects from the Southside, from 41st and Drexel.

While that lady was asking me questions about where I lived, there stood another woman and she was very large too, and had real large eyes. She was writing her address and phone number down for me, and she said, "*Here is my address and phone number*", and she said to me, "*I want you to come over and see me some times, alright*". She lived right in front of the church at 1520 West Hastings. The church address was 1517-19 West Hastings. So we left that church and went home to 1440 West 14th Street, Apt. 906. When we reached the building, my friends were waiting for me so we could drop off my daughter at my Mother's house. Doing this would make me free to go to Club Delices, even though the prayer of faith had been prayed over me. The Power of God had taken that load off my shoulder, yet I still went to that club with my friends. But let me say that things were not the same at that club. I did not feel the same, and the band could not reach me that evening, and it couldn't satisfy me. So someone said to me, "*Chrissy Baby, did you go to church today?*", and I said, "*You know I always go to church on Sunday*". Then someone said to me, "*What happened today at church?*", and I shouted, "*None of your business what happened!*" Not long after that, I said I wanted to go home. Thank You Jesus! And that was the last time that I ever went to a night club for anything. After that, I began to be by myself at home. Thank You Jesus!

So, one day after school was out, and Bernice was at my Mother's house, I was all alone as God began to speak to me. Thank You Lord Jesus! After that day, I began to act differently. I became so quiet that I could think. I began to put my playing cards in the incinerator. After that, I went to see that sanctified lady. Her name was Mrs. Cecelia Carpenter. I was not saved at the time, so I did not say Sister Carpenter. But when I went to see her, I would tell her more about God then I thought she knew. My Lord, I was so blind, but thanks be unto God! She would let me talk to her when I would leave her home. But the devil would say to me "*. . . you know more than she knows. None of these people are living right*", but I thank God for her kind and sweet spirit. Now I know what the scripture means when I read Jeremiah 31:3, "*The Lord hath appeared of old unto me, saying, Yea, I have loved thee with an everlasting love: therefore with lovingkindness have I drawn thee.*" That lady was very nice to me and she just let me talk to her, and she would say, "*I am glad for you*".

So, the morning God had saved me after I had repented with all my heart, I had come back to myself. I had a real large bath towel in my hand that I had buried my face in when I was crying out to God. It was very wet. I was sitting in the bathroom, and I was saying, *"Thank You Almighty God!"* And again I heard His voice saying unto me, *"Stand on your feet"*. So I stood with my face toward the medicine cabinet and the Lord said to me, *"Put on some clothing."* I began to do so. So, when I had finished putting on my clothes, I started to fix my hair and I heard the Lord say to me, *"Go!"* Before I could think, there appeared a straight path from my house to Sister Carpenter's house. I came out of the bathroom and picked up my door keys and went out the door. I took the elevator down to the first floor of the building where I lived, . . . 1440 South Loomis Street. I walked across the path to 1520 West 15th Street. When I got to the building, I took the elevator to the 14th floor, and went to apartment 1403. As I walked a few steps from the elevator, there came another voice, and it was the voice of the Lord. God said, *"Don't go in there, they don't have no more than you have."* But as

He's Sweet I Know

God continued to speak to me, I began to get afraid as though I was going to die. It was as if I was talking to someone, but I couldn't see them. With much speed, I went and knocked on that door anyway. I heard a voice saying to me, *"Who is it?"* I responded by saying, *"Ms. Christine Fields"*. She opened the door and said, *"Come in and have a seat. I will be with you in a little while."* She was getting her children ready to go back to school. I think it was a summer school, and they had come home for lunch. Nevertheless, when they left the house, she came and sat down and said to me, " . . . *tell me something!"* So, I began by saying how something happened to me.

I was sitting in my living room watching the TV and I got up to go to the bathroom. When I made a few steps, I heard a voice coming from within me saying, *"How long will you continue in your sins?"* That voice spoke to me three times. But the last time that voice spoke to me, it was so powerful. This time, God added by saying, *"Will you die for your sins?"* When I told Sister Carpenter what had happened to me, she said to me, *"Do you believe you are saved?"* With boldness, I said, *"No!, I know I am saved."* And she asked me, *"Have you ever been like this before?"* I said, "Yes!", ever since I was twelve years old. I didn't know, but I had *"religion"*. She said, *"What happened?"* I said, *"Well, I went out on the ballroom floor like many other Christians."* And she asked me, *"Do you know why?"* But before I could finish giving her my answer, she said to me, *"I know that you are just as saved as I am."*

Oh, I felt so good just to think that I am saved. My heart leaped for joy! Then she said, *"If you die right now, you would go to Heaven. But you are not going to die*". She said, "*. . . the Lord wants you to witness for Him. The reason why you did not stay saved was because you did not have the power*". Then I said, "*What do you mean? Do I have to get another religion?*" Then, she said, "*No! All you have to do is ask the Lord for the Holy Ghost. You can tarry now and the Lord will fill you with the Holy Ghost*". Then, I said, "*What else will I do?*" I began to ask her questions about the Holy Ghost. Everything I had outlined, I asked her, "*Can the Holy Ghost do it?*" She said, "*Yes!, and it will keep you until the Day of Redemption.*" That meant until Jesus comes back for His church. As I listened to her talk about Jesus, I said to her, "*. . . but when can I get that power?*" She said, "*Well, we do not have church tonight, but tomorrow you can come to the early Morning Prayer and Bible Class, and we will tarry with you. And the Lord will fill you*". I praise the Lord with the Holy Ghost!

She told me that the church doors would be opened at 7:00 o'clock in the morning. Prayer began at 7:00 a.m. and Bible Study starts at 9:00 a.m. Alright, I said when I left my sister's house. It looked like I was walking on air because everything was so beautiful to me. It had seemed as though the sun was shining at it fullest strength and the birds were singing and everybody that I saw looked good to me. I went straight to the record shop and bought a record by Brother Joe Mose. He was singing, "*I Don't Care What The World May Say, But I am Going Back to God.*"

He's Sweet I Know

My house was already cleaned, but I began to re-clean it. I had such a peace in my heart and mind. Thank You Jesus! I went to bed that night, and all through the night I was saying, *"Thank You Almighty God!"*

Early the next morning, I got out of bed and got dressed and went to the church. I went in the church and I found a lady in there praying. It was just one lady there, and her name was Evangelist Lula Williams. She lived in the basement of the church. When I saw her and the way she was praying, the devil spoke to me and said, **"You see that lady how she is looking, you will look just like her."** I believed to that day that the Lord told that lady to open her eyes. When she saw me, she got up and said to me, *"Good Morning!"*, and I said to her very sadly, *"Good Morning!"* I was very disappointed because that lady who I had visited was not there at that time. When Satan talks to you, it makes you feel bad. She said to me, *"Sit down."*, and I did, but I set on one side of the chair. I was discouraged because the lady who told me to come to church was not there.

The lady said to me, *"Are you saved?"*, and I said, *"Yes!, I m saved, but not like you all are."* Then I said to her, *"The other lady told me something about some Holy Ghost, and that's all I want."* Then she began to read scripture to me, Luke 11:9-13 and it said, *"And I say unto you, Ask, and it shall be given you; seek, and ye shall find; knock, and it shall be opened unto you. For everyone that asketh receiveth; and he that seeketh findeth; and to him that knocketh it shall be opened. If a son shall ask bread of any of you that is a father, will he give him a stone? Or if he ask a fish, will he for a fish give him a serpent? Or if he shall ask for an egg, will he offer him a scorpion? If ye then, being evil, know how to give good gifts unto your children: how much more shall your heavenly Father give the Holy Spirit to them that ask him?"*

When she finished reading that scripture, she asked, *"What is your father's name?"* I said, *"Joe Lark."* Then she said, *"Do you believe if you asked your father for bread that he would give you a stone?"* I said, *"No!"* Then she asked me, *"Well, do you believe that if you ask God for the Holy Ghost that He will give it to you?"* I said, *"I guess so."* And she said, *". . . that's not good enough."* Then she turned to the Book of Acts, the first Chapter, and began to read. Right at that time, the lady, Sister C. Carpenter came into the church. She said, *"I am so sorry that I did not tell you that I had to send my children to school."* When she spoke those words, I then turned around in the chair. Yes, I was willing to listen because I knew that she did not lie to me. Thank You Lord Jesus!

Evangelist Williams had got my attention in the work of God. When I didn't know anything, I was crying all over again and shaking. So, she said to me, *"Stop crying now!", and be glad because the Lord have already saved you."* I tried to do as she asked, but for a while, I just could not stop crying. So, she said to me, *"Come on now, and come with me"* So, she took me to the east end of the alter, and I began to tarry. She told me what to say, . . . *"Thank You Jesus!, . . . Thank You Jesus!"* After a while, I got so tired because I was saying the same thing over and over again. It felt like

He's Sweet I Know

my arms were going to fall off my shoulders. But I kept on saying, "*Thank You Jesus!, . . . Thank You Jesus!*", and the devil was telling me, "*. . . you are going to have a heart attack.*" I was so tired, but I could hear the voice of Evangelist Williams and Sister Carpenter saying to the Lord, "*Bless her Lord!*" I could hear Evangelist Williams saying to Satan, **"The Lord, Rebuke you from her mind!"** Then, I said to the Lord, "*If I did, then let me die!*" But because I was willing to die trying to get the Holy Ghost, I had made up in my mind to receive the power. Then all of a sudden, all I could see was a light around me, and it seemed like I was in a high place. Whatever it was, or wherever I was, it was like heaven. At that moment, I can say that I was there. "*Yes, Lord!, and I was at the feet of Jesus, . . . yet still saying, Thank You Jesus!, Thank You Jesus!*" I didn't know how long I had been away, but I did come back to myself, but I could still hear me saying, "*Glory to God!*" I had never heard me say those words before, Praise the Lord! When I went to the altar, there were only two people there. But when I had really come to myself, there were more people. There was Mother A. Morris, Mother C. Hace, Mother V. and Sister Louise Johnson. All these women were there at the altar, and they were beating on the tambourine, or should I say playing the tambourine and singing songs of deliverance. Thank God!, I had been delivered by God's Holy power. I tried to fix my clothes so I could look decent. After that, Mother Morris said to me, "*Tell us, daughter what the Lord had did for you?*" Before I could say very much of anything, the devil told me, **"Don't tell me that you got the Holy Ghost?"** All I could say was,

"*He, . . . He, . . . He* blessed *me.*" Then Mother Morris said, "*Saints, the Lord has blessed this daughter, and the devil is telling her not to tell it.*" Oh my Lord, for someone to say just what the devil was saying to me was terrifying. But when I went back to the altar this time, they didn't have to say anything to me because my mouth was wide open. They said that I preached all over the church, Thank You Jesus! I have not been the same since that day.

I truly thank God for this church, First Pentecostal Church of God. God has blessed me down through the years. In 1963, the Lord blessed me to marry our Bishop and Pastor of this great work, the late Bishop James Morris. Bishop Morris was a wonderful Man of God. We got married on December 15, 1963 at 4:00p.m. The Lord had kept me for seven years. I thank God because I had been saved for seven, too. When I first received the Lord in His fullness, I made some mistakes. But as I followed the Lord, I became stronger, Thank God! The Lord blessed me to work as our Bishop's Co-Pastor for twelve years.

After his death, I became the Pastor of the First Pentecostal Church of God, Inc. Of course, our Bishop called a business meeting and told the church members that I would be the Pastor of the church if he did not come back from the hospital. So, when he got ready to go to the hospital, he said to them, "*My wife is the Pastor.*" When I go to the hospital to visit him, it would be on a service night, and he would say to me, "*Honey, go home now so you can be at church with the saints, and carry on.*" So, I said to him, "*Honey, I can *leave before 8:00p.m., so I could be in the service with the saints."*

Lord, I thank You for my husband and his first wife because the both of them was so good to me. She taught me before she died, and because of her teachings, I have been able to teach women, especially young women how to love and live their lives' as Women of God.

I thank God for my teachings!

Apostle's Notes

January 9, 2005

"Today is the second Sunday of January 2005. I am praising God, the Father of our Lord and Saviour Jesus Christ for His many blessings to me. He has blessed me with my family and my church, the First Pentecostal Church of God, Inc. I am truly giving all the glory and honor to the Lord for what He has done 'Down Through the Years' in this great church. First of all, God did a wonderful work in the beginning through two great servants of this church; the late Bishop James Morris and Mother Ardella Morris. For forty years, our Bishop has lead the people of God in true holiness. In 1981, the Lord called our Bishop James Morris home to be with Him, and rest from his labor. I thank God because his work shall follow him."

February 14, 2005

"This is Dr. Christine Morris, the Apostle of the First Pentecostal Church of God, Inc. at 5146 South Ashland Avenue. I am praising the Lord this day for saving me, . . . healing me, . . . keeping me, . . . and filling me with the Holy Ghost, . . . oh Praise God! I have been sick up and down beginning in the month of September. I began going to the doctor more and more, traveling back and forth to Little Company of Mary Hospital. Before I began getting weak, I smashed my car because

my eyes was failing me so I began loosing my way of getting around, and that brought on more pressure. Because of this, I want you all to know that the trials had began to come on more and more while I was fighting the good fight of faith. Because I was lacking of spiritual strength from those that were here to support the ministry on my behalf, I was holding on to my job as the Overseer of my ministry, Speak The Truth. I am a little sad, but I am thinking about something. I am witnessing in the church, and I am praying that God will help me to keep my heart, my mind and my hands clean and pure because Holiness is the only way I see God. What I witnessed tonight, I have never seen it like this before.

The church asked to help me celebrate my birthday by serving cake, ice cream and punch. Well, I had no punch, no spoon, no fork to eat with, and no tablecloths on the table, one bottle of water and no glass to drink from. No song was sung to me on my birthday with no family and friends. I became discouraged because I did not ask anything for myself before and I don't want to start. Now I have always thought about this because what I do and when I do, I do it with my whole heart because anything that is done must be done out of pure love, and not just to be seen or heard. I would not have gone downstairs if I had known that the table was not set up for me. I asked someone where was I going to sit. The beautiful cakes were still in the boxes, and there were no napkins on the table. I had never seen anything like this before at anybody's celebration. I was so ashamed that I became sick to my stomach. My heart was sad. It never happened again. But on top of all this, they had small children scooping up ice cream and passing it out, and there was still no punch at all. So, I say, Lord, whatever happened in my life, please let me not fall in the hands of men. Understand, sometimes it is good to tell people just how bad you are feeling about what is going on around you."

April 6, 2005

" Tonight I talked with my baby granddaughter, Evangelist Marcie Williams, and she brought peace to my mind. Because I was being vexed in my thoughts, I mean very oppressed, I was feeling sorry for myself. I was worrying over what I cannot do in life. But I should be thinking about the things that I can do so I can give God the glory. Evangelist Marcie did not rebuke me, but she shared something with me, . . . something that is the very truth, . . . that God is Able!"

May 10, 2006

"My name is Apostle Christine Morris, the Overseer of the First Pentecostal Church. I was the pastor of this church for about twenty-five years. I became the pastor after the death of my husband, Bishop James Morris. But before he went into the hospital, he released the pastorship into my hands. So, tonight, May 10, I am looking back over my work as pastor. When I think about how God has blessed me, and the work of God, all I can say and all I want to say is, 'Blessed the name of our Lord and Saviour Jesus Christ because all that

happened to me. God did it! Tuesday was my birthday, and the Lord blessed me to reach my seventy-ninth birthday, and I give the Lord all the praise and all the glory. I am writing a few things this morning. It is about 3:45 a.m."

July 18, 2007 – 4:00.am.

"My name is Christine Morris, and I am a child of God. Because God saved me in nineteen fifty-seven, and I thank the Lord! I had a stroke in January 2006, and God sent His Word and healed me, and God gave me strength in my limbs. God blessed me to have one daughter, Bernice whom I have always respected and have always loved my only child. I always wanted the very best for her and her children, and also my great-grandchildren. Truly I love everyone of them, Bernice's oldest son Reggie Williams who had four beautiful children: two girls and two boys who I have shown love to them all their lives. I love and respect each one of them. Reggie is gone by the way of the grave. But as I look back over my life this morning, I thank God and give Him the praises for His goodness to me and my church because the Lord has kept me on my feet and closed in my right mind as I tried to lead God's people. But as I became weaker and weaker in my body, my strength began to fail me more and more, and I was going back and forth to the hospital and I was not getting any better. My whole left side began to pain me night and day. My daughter, Bernice came home for New Year's Service, and she brought the Word of God. Then she stayed over my house for a few days. When

she was here, she took me to my doctor, and then she took me to the hospital, but I was not getting any better. But I thank God because He knew what He was doing by setting my daughter up to become the new pastor of this church and carry on the work of this vision."

AWARDS AND ACCOMPLISHMENTS

Since then, God has blessed Pastor with the gift of healing (via blinded eyes, cancer, AIDS, drug addictions and many others). Through her tenure as Pastor, God has blessed her with many accomplishments:

- One of the first wives to become Co-Pastor to her husband
- Started the First Women's Day Service in the church, and later to become a Three-Day Convention
- Continued the Sunrise Easter Morning Breakfast Fellowship from 1964-2001
- Consecrated as Pastor of the First Pentecostal Church of God, Inc. by Apostle Richard D. Henton.
- Provided food for the homeless and Elderly during Thanksgiving
- Started the First Nursery in the church
- Taught Tuesday Night and Every Morning Bible Class for over 40 years
- Ordained and Counsel Pastors, Bishops, Apostles and Clergyman across the country
- Received her Doctorate Degree in 1991 from Trinity College
- Consecrated into Apostleship in 2001

- Dedicated over 30 Churches and Ministries in and around the Chicagoland area and one ministry in St John, Virgin Islands
- Founder and Visionary of the "*Speak the Truth Fellowship*" which started with 17 churches.
- Founder of the First P School of Ministry which began in January 2004
- "*Pioneer In the Gospel*" recipient at the 100th Year Celebration of Azusa-2006

Apostle Morris is the mother of one daughter, Dr. Bernice Williams (current Pastor of First Pentecostal Church of God), four grandchildren, eight great grandchildren, and four great-great grandchildren.

Because God has been so good to me, I just continue to give Him all the praise and all the glory and honor for my life. When I truly look back over my life, I can truly testify and say, "*I Don't Know What I Would Do Without The Lord*". God has kept me "*Down Through The Years*" . . .

. . . and that's why to me, *"He's Sweet I know"*.